The **D**ivorce **R**esource **S**eries

No Easy Answers

A Teen Guide to Why Divorce Happens

Florence Calhoun

THE ROSEN PUBLISHING GROUP, INC.
NEW YORK

Published in 2000 by The Rosen Publishing Group, Inc.
29 East 21st Street, New York, NY 10010

First Edition

Library of Congress Cataloging-in-Publication Data

Calhoun, Florence.
   No easy answers: a teen guide to why divorce happens/ Florence Calhoun.
     p. cm.— (The divorce resource series)
   Includes bibliographical references and index.
   Summary: Focuses on the thoughts and feelings of teenagers who are experiencing their parents' divorce and offers guidance as to how to respond and what to expect from the situation.
   ISBN 0-8239-3153-6
   1. Divorce— Juvenile literature. 2. Broken homes— Juvenile literature. 3. Children of divorced parents— Juvenile literature. 4. Parent and teenager— Juvenile literature. [1. Divorce. 2. Parent and teenager.] I.Title. II. Series.

HQ814.C32 2000
306.89—dc21
                                        99-039558

Manufactured in the United States of America

Contents

Introduction

A divorce is the legal end of a marriage. Over the past several years, millions of people in the United States—spouses and children—have faced divorce. Statistics indicate varying rates of divorce. The most commonly cited statistic indicates that one in every four families will face divorce.

Divorce occurs often, and it can happen to anyone. Parents decide to seek divorce for many reasons. No two family situations are exactly the same.

One reason for divorce is that people change, and individuals are sometimes unable to address or adjust to the changes. Another is that people become dissatisfied

One in every four families will face divorce in the United States.

and can no longer find peace and contentment in their marriage. Whatever the reason might be, the entire family suffers, each member in his or her own individual way. A divorce is a parting of the ways for children as well as for parents, grandparents, cousins, aunts, uncles, even friends of the family. Everyone's life changes in one way or another.

With a divorce, there are many issues to settle, especially for children. Often a change in residence becomes a major issue, as does the question of which parent is going to have the primary responsibility to care for the child. The emotional trauma involved can be devastating, although it does not have to be. Divorce is a disruption of the familiar, normal flow of one's life, and it is unsettling for all who experience it.

If your parents have decided to divorce, you will experience all kinds of feelings and think all kinds of thoughts. You might want to talk over your concerns with someone. Maybe you want to ask someone for answers to your questions or just want to share your concerns with someone you think will understand. Often teens find it difficult to share their feelings openly, and you might also. Maybe you are too embarrassed or think no one will understand your feelings. You are aware that divorce happens to others, but you did not think it would ever happen to you. You might wonder how your life could be turned upside down so quickly and why there does not seem to be anything that you can do about it. Most of all, you are likely to wonder how and why this could happen.

This book is intended to provide you with support and answers to some of the disturbing questions that you might have about divorce. It is also intended to illustrate ways you can survive the disappointment and realize that though your life will change, you can have a positive and loving relationship with both your parents. Though there is no denying that divorce represents an end to certain things in your life, it can be the beginning of positive new things as well.

CHAPTER 1

When Divorce Happens

Brian, age fifteen, did not know whether his parents would actually get divorced, but he was not surprised when he learned that they were separating.

Brian; his older sister, Becky, age sixteen; and his younger brother, Kevin, age eight, had sensed bitterness and hostility between their parents for years. When their father lost his job, the family suffered financially. Life at home became unstable and insecure, filled with chaos and confusion. Their parents fought constantly, and the arguments became increasingly bitter.

Brian responded by spending as much time away from home as possible. His absence from home and his choice of friends became another source of discontentment between his parents, and they began to blame each other for Brian's behavior.

It may be difficult to stay inside your home while your parents are fighitng

Finally, his mother decided to leave his father and move away to live with her parents in another state about a thousand miles away.

Long-Term Hostility Between Parents

Though Brian was disappointed by his parents' decision, he was not totally surprised. He was somewhat prepared. At least he had known that his parents were not happy. Often teens will see that their parents are not getting along, but they might hold on to the hope that they will work out their differences. Brian obviously did not like the fighting between them and was hurt by the instability and uncertainty of their lives, but he did not like the thought of the breakup either.

You might react to your situation in one way, but someone else might react in quite another. As the fighting and hostility between Brian's parents grew, so did his sense of discontentment with the family's situation. A home should be a place of shelter, love, and security. These qualities were not available to Brian. The lack of these essential ingredients for a stable home life affected the entire household.

It is extremely difficult for children to witness long-term fighting and hostility between parents, the two people on whom children rely to provide their most basic needs. During this time in a teen's life, he or she is likely to be going through tremendous physiological, social, and emotional changes independent of whatever their parents are experiencing. You are involved in the business of growing up, engaging in the normal and natural changes of this stage of your development. Males and females have passed through puberty and are beginning to establish themselves socially. For most teens, how their peers view them is very important. You are finding your own identity while exploring relationships with the opposite sex. This can be very disturbing and made even more difficult when you are simultaneously being confronted with the breakup of your family. It seems to say that even the deepest romantic relationships are impermanent, hurtful, and even destructive.

During this difficult period, most teens experience a number of conflicting thoughts and feelings. When your parents argue, you want to put as much distance between you and them as you possibly can. You might wonder why you sometimes want to scream and run out of the house. You might wonder why you feel as though you want to take charge of your own life. You might feel as though you want to take over the leadership role from your parents. In one sense, you might feel more grown up than them because your parents, in your eyes, are no longer acting reasonably.

Brian chose to distance himself by finding a family away from home. This family away from home was a substitute, or surrogate, for his real family. He found friends that would accept him and make him feel that he belonged. He began to stay out late at night, not letting his parents know where he was going or when he would return. He wanted to be independent and run his own life. Brian was suffering, but he did not know why or how to effectively deal with his pain. For a long time he had suffered in silence when his parents argued. The months and years of witnessing hostility between his parents had hardened him; yet, they did not erase his yearning for closeness and belonging.

It is normal for teens to be somewhat preoccupied with their own feelings and needs. The normal physiological, social, and emotional changes that teens undergo during these years require the support and wisdom of parents if healthy development is to occur. When parents are distracted by their own problems, they may find it difficult to provide such support. For teens, this can cause conflicting feelings and changes (sometimes dramatic changes) in behavior, which is called acting out.

When Divorce Happens Suddenly

In contrast to Brian's situation, the decision to separate can happen quite suddenly in some families, leaving the children totally unprepared and causing shock and dismay. When divorce in their family happens suddenly, teens naturally wonder what will happen to them and whether their lives will ever be normal again.

Karen, age sixteen, a junior in high school, was totally surprised when her parents told her they were getting a divorce. Karen and her younger sister, Meg, age thirteen, were both happy, popular girls. Karen played on the girls' basketball team and was very involved in her church. She worked extremely hard to earn decent grades in school. Meg was close to her older sister and tried to follow her example. Both were close to their parents, whom they believed loved each other deeply. Neither child had any idea that the marriage was in trouble. Obviously their parents had their differences, as Meg and Karen found out, but they were able to keep from arguing in front of their children.

Their parents broke the news to the girls one evening after dinner. The girls' dad revealed that he wanted a change and that he would be moving out of the house. He had already told his wife that he had fallen in love with the woman with whom he had been having an affair for the past few months. Both parents explained the hopelessness of their marriage. They announced that the divorce was certain.

The fear of the unknown is common to all humans. All of us fear change, and divorce brings many changes. When news of a divorce arrives as a sudden announcement, it can be a profound shock to your emotions and may produce an immediate feeling of uncertainty and a lack of confidence and hope for the future.

The fear of change gripped Karen so tightly that she began to fall apart in many ways. She found herself unwilling or unable to talk to either of her parents or confide in anyone at school. Her situation was so overwhelming to her that she found it difficult to study or take part in any of her normal activities. She lost interest in the things that had been most important to her before and that had seemed such a natural part of her personality. Her grades dropped, and she no longer associated with her friends. Sadness, fear, and loneliness seemed to take over completely.

Although Brian was somewhat prepared for his parents' separation and Meg and Karen were not, these teens had a couple of important things in common. They were both deeply affected by what was happening in their families, and their responses were completely natural and understandable under the circumstances. This is not the same thing as saying that they were the only possible responses or that all the pain these teens experienced was absolutely inevitable.

CHAPTER 2

The Conflicting Feelings of Divorce

Separation or divorce causes a level of grief similar to any other loss. Any reaction to loss includes a set of specific emotional responses and behaviors that together constitute what psychologists, therapists, and social workers sometimes call the stages of grief. In this view, grief is not a single, distinct emotion but a process of working through loss. For a child, the divorce of his or her parents can be one of the most profound losses the child can experience. Experts who specialize in emotional health associate specific behaviors and feelings with each stage.

Denial

When you first realize that your parents are going to separate or divorce, your immediate response might be disbelief. You might not want to believe it, or you might wish that it would not happen. You might go around telling yourself that you do not really care, that it does not matter one way or the other, or that you are not going to show anyone how much it hurts. These responses can be positive or negative, depending on such factors as their duration and extremity—that is, how long these feelings last, how intense they are, and how you act them out. Denial is a way of easing the pain that you are feeling. Denial is our way of protecting ourselves from what we believe will be a dreadful experience. To a certain extent this works. However, when denial stops you from reaching any of the other stages, even more serious problems can result.

Meg, Karen's sister, was in denial about her parents' divorce. While Karen responded with withdrawal and depression, Meg continued to go on with her activities as before. It appeared as though she was okay. If any-one asked how she was doing, Meg's answer was always the same: "Fine." While her sister struggled, Meg dug deeper into her school activities than she ever had before. Pretending, for her own protection, that everything was the same, Meg became compulsive about her activities and her school work. She mini-mized, or made light of, her feelings of loss.

Many people regard carrying on in the face of a profound loss, as if nothing has happened, to be brave or courageous. In many ways it is or can be. However, when such behavior prevents you from accessing all your feelings about the loss, even greater long-term problems can result.

Bargaining

Bargaining is another stage in the grieving process. Like most people, teens will do anything to avoid having their lives turned upside down and experiencing the pain of loss. Who wouldn't, right?

Brian's older sister, Becky, knew in her heart that her parents' divorce was the best outcome—for them, for her, and for her brothers. Even so, she began to "bargain" with her parents to keep them together, as if by behaving in a certain way she could change the decision they had made. She began to do things that she thought would make her parents' life together less stressful. She began to clean the house regularly, from top to bottom, without being asked to do so. She became more cooperative and responsible about looking after her little brother, and she did many special things for her parents. Through her actions, Becky was trying to say, "If you stay together, I will help make things better around here." Unconsciously, she was asking herself, "What can I do to stop this?"

Younger children often think that their parents are divorcing because of them. Even though older children may know that the divorce has nothing to do with them, they may have some lingering feelings of guilt. "If I had been different, if I had been better," children sometimes feel, "my parents might still be together." Younger children promise to change their ways or "be good"; teens will try to intervene in other ways, as Becky did.

Anger

When you experience an emotional shock, anger is a common response. You may wonder why your parents got married in the first place. You may get mad because you feel like a victim. Victims feel helpless because bad things have happened

Younger children often think that if they promise to be good, their parents won't get a divorce.

to them that they did not cause and that they cannot remedy. Everyone likes to feel that he or she has control over his or her life. You may be angry because you know that your life will change, and in the beginning stages of the divorce, you may not be sure what this change will mean in your life. The following are typical ways that teens express their anger:

- ✤ Not eating
- ✤ Acting rebellious
- ✤ Not sleeping well
- ✤ Changing study habits
- ✤ Hanging out with new people
- ✤ Experimenting with new behavior, such as tobacco, alcohol, and drugs

Sadness

Sadness is a natural response to learning that your parents are splitting up. The underlying causes for your feelings are easy to understand. For example, you recognize that your relationship with your parents will be different. You know that you will have to leave one parent to live with another. You feel sad for your parents, too, because you care about them and you know what they are going through makes them very sad. You know that your life will never be the same again, and that thought makes you very sad. It is important to be honest with yourself about these feelings. They are quite normal. If you do not face them, they will find a resting place somewhere within you and, sometime in the future, interfere with healthy emotional responses to other situations.

Fear

If you know that you have to go someplace that you have never been to before, and you have heard nothing but bad things about it, it is understandable that you might be afraid. It is much the same with learning that your parents are separating. In a way, the news means that you will be going somewhere that you

Teens may express their anger about divorce by experimenting with drugs and alcohol.

have never been, and everyone has certainly heard a lot of negative things about life after divorce.

It is very common to fear the unknown, and fear of the unknown can be more terrifying than actually experiencing it. When you are able to face this feeling and tell others how you feel, you will find that it is not as difficult as you might have thought. You will learn that others have had similar feelings and experiences. You will learn how they managed to cope with those feelings. Fear is a normal and natural response during the early stages of a family's breakup. Your parents are scared, too. Sensing their fear can cause you to feel even more insecure.

Blame

When something bad happens, it is natural to look for an explanation. It is unsettling to think that things can just happen and that there is sometimes little or nothing that you can do about it. So you look for a reason and, sometimes, someone to blame.

If the divorce is sudden, the parent who leaves is the one who is usually blamed. In the case of long-standing arguments, complaints, and bickering, blame goes from one parent to the other on a regular basis. Children often see blame for the situation first expressed by their parents, whom they may have seen openly argue and blame each other.

Younger children often blame themselves for the divorce. Teens, even though they know that they did not cause the problem, sometimes blame themselves for not being able to stop it from happening. You might find yourself caught up in this blaming game. You might blame one parent or the other for not preventing it.

Acceptance

At last, if a teen is able to work through these feelings and stages, he or she will reach the stage of acceptance. At this point, teens have resigned themselves to the fact that their parents are splitting up. There is no definite time period for each of these stages. Some teens will stay in the denial stage longer than others will. Some may reach the acceptance stage before others. The point here is to understand that there is a normal process of getting through this very difficult period in your life.

CHAPTER 3

Taking Sides

When parents separate or divorce, children find themselves in an extremely awkward position. They have, up to that point, shared their love and loyalty equally between both parents. Divorce can force them to divide their loyalty, which can result in a new set of conflicting feelings and emotions.

It can be difficult for children of divorcing parents to remain loyal to both parents. When your parents are together, you feel a sense of balance, togetherness, and unity. You have the sense that everyone feels the same way about each other. It is normal for teens who are aware of the circumstances leading to the divorce, whether they are sudden or long-term problems, to struggle with their feelings regarding the divorce or separation.

Children might side with the parent to whom they feel closer or they might side with the parent they feel has been wronged in the process. Yet as children take sides, another conflict can develop in the form of guilt about favoring one parent over the other. When this happens, they may blame one or both parents for these feelings.

After learning of her parents' divorce, Karen became withdrawn to the point that she found it impossible to take sides. The most she felt capable of was wishing that the whole thing would go away. She empathized with her mother's pain and disappointment, and she felt anger toward her father for his actions. Yet it was too painful for her to side with either parent. So she became a passive bystander, which only made her feel more powerless and depressed. Although it seems normal and natural to identify with the parent who you think has been wronged, this is not such an easy thing to do; it is difficult to align yourself with one parent against the other. For Karen, siding with her mother would have meant siding against her father, and this was too difficult for her to do.

The Different Developmental Needs of Male and Female Teens

During the teen years, males and females are in the process of separating themselves from their parents.

Children may feel they have to side with one parent during divorce.

Mothers and fathers have different roles to play in the successful physical, social, and emotional development of their children at this time. Both parents influence their sons and daughters in different and important ways.

Though children derive natural and necessary benefits from their parent of the same sex (girls and their mother, boys and their father), a close relationship with the parent of the opposite sex helps the teen to successfully make the separation that is required in this stage of development.

Karen may not have realized it or been able to express it, but she may have been angry with her mother for not doing more to keep her father from leaving. She needed the help of her father, even after the divorce, to help her resolve some of the conflicts she had with her mother.

Brian was close to his father and needed him for guidance and support. Yet his mother played a necessary role in helping him learn how to deal with and have successful relationships with the opposite sex.

Brian was angry with both of his parents for not being able to work out their differences and for not being available to him. He was angry with his mother for moving away from the place where he had lived all his life. He was also angry over being put in a position

Choosing who to live with after a divorce can cause you to become upset with your parents

of having to choose between his parents regarding his place of residence. Brian felt additional pressure because he anticipated that he might now be asked to act as the man of the house. He was uncomfortable with that possibility. He did not feel ready for that responsibility and resented his parents for putting him in that position.

Outsiders

In a divorce, there is another element of taking sides that often affects children. Unless the parents are able to reach an agreement themselves on all the elements of the divorce, outside professionals often become involved. These can include lawyers, judges, therapists, psychologists, social workers, and other mediators and health care professionals. Dealing with your feelings by yourself is difficult enough; being asked to share them with strangers and outsiders can be nearly impossible.

The most common situation wherein teens and other children have direct contact with such professionals is when their parents cannot agree over who will have custody of the children. Custody is often thought of as determining with which parent the child will live, but it is actually the legal responsibility for raising and providing for the child. If one parent is given custody, generally the other has visitation rights.

When divorcing parents cannot agree over who will have responsibility for taking care of their children, a judge in a court of law makes the decision for them. Custody is often the most contentious issue in a divorce case.

In deciding which parent is to be given custody, judges often try to determine what would be in the best interest of the child. However, in most states, there is no law that sets specific standards that judges have to use in such cases.

For many years, the presumption was that the mother was the best parent to be assigned the responsibility for raising the children, unless she has proven to be negligent or abusive in the past. Under this assumption, the most important role of the father was the economic supporter of the family. Thus, the most common outcome of custody disputes was that the mother would be assigned custody of the child and the father would be assigned to pay the mother a certain amount for the economic support of the child.

Although this is still the most common outcome, in the last two decades an increasing number of fathers have received custody. Joint custody, in which parents share the responsibilities, has also become much more common.

Do children have to take sides in a custody dispute? Emotionally, it is often difficult not to. However, it is rare that a child, especially a younger child, would be made to testify in court, in front of a judge, about which parent he or she would prefer to live with. What is more likely to happen is that a professional assigned by the court—usually a psychologist, therapist, or social worker—will interview the child about his or her home life and his or her feelings about the situation, then issue a report to the court. The judge may or may not make his decision about custody based on the recommendations in such reports.

In such situations, children may feel less like they are taking sides than that they are being torn apart emotionally by love for and loyalty to both parents. In such situations, it is important that children find someone to help them deal with their emotions. Ideally, this should not be a professional appointed by a court or someone who is working on the behalf of one of their parents in the custody matter. What children need is someone whose only interest is what is best

A judge in family court will make a decision about custody based on many facts for them, which is not always what is best for the parents. How children can find adults who can help them in such situations will be discussed later in this book.

When Mom Leaves

Sometimes when parents begin to have marital difficulties, the mother leaves first. This usually adds to the teen's stress over the family's breakup. Traditionally, the mother is the one who provides the glue that binds the family together. Legally, this is reflected in the presumption that, in most cases, the mother is the one who should have custody. However, certain circumstances dictate the hard choices that parents sometimes make.

More divorced fathers are beginning to raise children alone. Single mothers, too, can and do raise families successfully. As long as teens have a secure home headed by a responsible, supportive, and caring parent, they will most likely be assured of healthy development.

When Brian's mother told him that she was moving away and that she wanted all the children to come with her, he was sad, confused, and angry. A part of him felt that he should stay with his father because, in spite of the family's history, he felt close to him. It saddened him to think of his father living all alone. Even though he had rebelled against his parents, he realized he loved both of them and found it difficult to separate from either of them.

So what did he do? He tried to sort out his thinking about the choice that he had to make. He thought about the consequences and issues involved with leaving or staying. He felt that if he stayed, he could keep his friends, attend the same school, and perhaps have even more freedom than he had with his mother. On the other hand, he would miss his mom and his sister and brother. Going with his mom, of course, would keep the family together. However, he might risk endangering the relationship that he had with his father. He was afraid of hurting either parent, yet he was unable to discuss his feelings with any of the professionals the court had assigned to the case. Brian ran away and remained in hiding among his friends for six weeks.

It is normal for children to want their parents to stay together. Perhaps Brian's running away was his way of trying to let his parents know how he felt. It may also have been an attempt to delay, or stall, the process in the hope that they would stay together. He felt guilty because he believed the family was abandoning his father. Brian's father had lost his job, and the family income had dwindled to half what it had been. Even though his mother told him she would be able to get a better job, he was

Sometimes when parents begin to have marital difficulties, the mother leaves first.

nevertheless concerned about the family's situation, wondering whether or not they would be able to survive. These are common concerns that all children have when their parents are separating or divorcing.

When Dad Leaves

Karen was devastated over the breakup of her family and suffering from the immediate shock of learning about it. Another aspect of her grief was her knowledge of the impact that her father's leaving would have on the family.

Karen's mother worked only part-time and earned very little money. Karen feared that the financial burden her mother would have to face would be overwhelming. Karen had little knowledge about child support or alimony. These financial questions

Often the financial concerns of your parents divorce can seem devastating.

caused her a great deal of fear and anxiety. She worried that their lives would change drastically and feared that her mother would be forced to get a full-time job. Her mother had been ill, and Karen thought that she would find it difficult to work full-time.

Karen wondered if they would have to move to a smaller place, or whether they would have to leave the area altogether. These are unknowns that are commonly felt during the early stages of the divorce process. During this stage, when your feelings are still very new and intense and you are not quite sure how to deal with them, it is important to talk over your thoughts and feelings with someone.

Getting Out of the Middle

It is uncomfortable to be in the middle of the emotions involved in your parents' separation. Adolescents choose a variety of ways to stay out of the middle. Some parents help their teens by shielding them from their own conflicts as much as possible.

For some parents, however, the process is more overwhelming, and their children inevitably are brought into the middle it. Parents use various tactics to engage their teens in the conflict. Some parents unwittingly seek the help of their teens to support them in the conflict and sometimes use their children to gain information about the activities of the other spouse. These tactics can prove extremely detrimental to teens in the long run and make the early stage of the divorce or separation process even more difficult.

In emotional terms, Karen chose to get out of the middle by withdrawing totally. Although it is understandable, it is clear that in many ways this was not the best decision for her. She became disconnected from her parents and lost within herself. She was unable to resolve any of the inner conflicts that she felt or the conflicts involving the breakup of her family. She needed to find a way to remain connected to both parents but disconnected from their conflict.

Sometimes adolescents take on the responsibility of trying to help their parents work things out. This, of course, produces more anxiety and stress and keeps you in the middle of the conflict. Why do parents divorce? There are probably as many different reasons as there are divorces. One thing is for certain, though: It is never the child's fault or the child's responsibility. Parents divorce or separate for their own reasons, and they must work through the conflict in their own way.

When the normal flow and structure of the family breaks down, adolescents often attempt to take on adult responsibilities. Although it is admirable to act as grown-up as possible about any situation, teens are not adults, and they should not expect themselves to resolve, handle, or deal with adult problems. Very few adults handle divorce well, so their children should not be surprised if they find themselves overwhelmed at times. The best thing to do is to admit that the situation can be overwhelming, then take it from there.

Brian found himself squarely in the middle of his parents' problems. He wanted to help, as teens often do in such situations. When he found he could not fix the problem, he blamed himself rather than realizing that only his parents could solve their problems. In response, he withdrew and rebelled.

When he was a child, his parents' arguments had made him afraid. As a teenager, he felt anger and resentment. Yet a part of him felt that he could help. He got involved in the arguments, trying to understand why his parents were not able to get along. He would talk to his parents separately, but his efforts to mediate their conflict brought him too close to their disagreements. Ultimately, this only made their separation more difficult for him to accept.Brian had to learn how to separate himself from his parents' conflicts.

CHAPTER 4

Moving On

Although there is no denying that divorce can be an extremely difficult experience in a variety of ways, it does not have to be altogether a bad thing. In its different stages, it can cause a great deal of anguish. However, the initial period of shock and confusion does pass, and loving relationships between family members can and do resume. These relationships will be different in some ways than before, but different does not always mean worse. In some ways and in certain circumstances, divorce can make family relationships better.

This does not happen automatically, of course. It requires understanding, acceptance of the new way of life that will emerge, and careful communication among family members. In some cases, this kind of communication is a skill that family members need to learn, both individually and together. In the best case, you will begin to understand some of the positive outcomes of the breakup. You will learn to see each of your parents in a very different light. Though you learned to view them for the most part as a team, you will get to know them as individuals. With some resolution to the difficulties that separated them, your parents may have more energy and time to put into their relationship with you.

You can draw new meanings from your relationship with each parent. You will broaden your horizons through the expansion of friendships and associations. Your parents will maintain some of their old friendships while they form new ones. You will learn how to adjust to these changed relationships and increase your level of maturity. Your life may actually become more stable without some of the conflicts that were present in the earlier stages of divorce or separation, allowing you to see your present and future more clearly.

Your own personality will emerge. You will begin to feel like your old self again. You will find that part of you is different and part of you is the same. It will seem as though you have traveled through a dark tunnel and met danger along the way, and now you

are outside in the bright sunshine again, feeling fairly safe and secure. The past is a part of you, but you welcome the present and it is beginning to feel okay.

No More Noise

Brian was quite aware of the peace and quiet that had entered into his life. He and his brother and sister no longer winced at the loud, angry voices and words that left them sad and bitter at the same time. They stopped worrying that anything they did or said might get one of their parents angry and that the result would inevitably be a fight. They found a greater sense of inner peace and quiet.

Eventually you will begin to feel like your old self again.

Brian decided that he wanted to remain with his father. His brother and sister, meanwhile, went to live with their mother. Since they lived so far away, the plan was that Brian would see his mother and siblings during the summer months and on special holidays like Thanksgiving and Christmas.

Brian's adjustment to his new life was slow and somewhat rocky in the beginning, but with the help of others, it began to improve. Brian began to be more open to the support that had been offered to him. His school counselor ran a support group for children whose parents had recently divorced, and Brian found this group to be helpful. Fellow students led the group, so he was listening to voices of experience. Brian found in the group an avenue to express his feelings to an accepting and understanding peer group. Brian's father became more available to him and appeared to be happy and more content with his life. He was able to listen to Brian and share some of his own feelings. Thus, Brian saw his father as more human and became more accepting of him.

Brian missed his mother and siblings greatly, of course. His mother telephoned him often, and they wrote letters to each other frequently. They made plans for when they would see each other again and discussed other important issues in their lives. Although he missed the day-to-day contact, in some ways Brian found it easier to communicate with his

mother now. There was simply less tension in the air. Through this frequent communication, they learned about each other's lives and maintained the continuity of family ties.

As things settled down for him and his fears about the future eased a little bit, Brian was able to resume positive relationships with friends and no longer felt compelled to act out in negative ways. He also found it easy to make new friends when he visited his mother and brother and sister.

Brian and his family did not work out this friendly state of affairs entirely on their own. In time the family was able to realize the benefit of the professional help they had received from counselors and therapists. They worked at incorporating into their new lives what they had learned about themselves and what they wanted for their future. The result was a fairly positive adjustment for the entire family after a long, bitter marital relationship.

With professional help, Karen, too, was able to move on. Probably because of the sudden nature of the separation and later divorce, Karen, her sister, and their mother had a more difficult time healing. The girls received individual counseling and family counseling with their mother. Family counseling sometimes involved their father. With help and time they were able to restore the

It is important to keep up communication when your family seperates.

loving relationship they had shared with their parents before the problems began.

Individual counseling helped Karen to get over her depression. She began to have a better understanding of how to cope with her circumstances. She learned that it was okay to love both her parents. The anger that she felt toward her father began to diminish.

In her own counseling, Karen's sister, Meg, was able to talk about her feelings concerning what was happening to her family. She developed a better understanding of why she had suddenly become so driven and why she seemed to have such a need to keep moving. She settled back into a normal pace. Noise in the form of disruption, negative feelings, sudden hostility, and anger subsided. The family members found a new way of relating to each other.

Communication Is the Key

Both families learned that communicating openly and honestly was the key to calming their fears and easing the burdens of their changing lifestyle. Through honest communication, the teens came to better understand some of the reasons why their parents chose to separate.

Until they were able to talk to each other about what was happening to them, the teens could only question and guess about what was going to happen to them, and the questioning and guessing caused inner conflict and confusion. Communication opened doors to improved understanding of how they would live their lives apart from a parent or siblings. This opening up helped the parents, as well, to develop a better vision for their future. Teens need to know that their parents love them and want to continue to guide them and make life as good as it can be. Hearing this directly from their parents reassures them and gives them comfort and confidence in their future.

Your New Life

Adjusting to your life will have its high moments and its low moments. You may have to adjust to many new things: a new relationship with your parents, a new home, new friends, and a new community, for instance. You may be saying good-bye to old friends and having to find new ways to maintain those friendships. You will also be learning to adjust to new relationships in your parents' lives. The latter is probably one of the most difficult adjustments of all.

New Relationships with Parents

Even though your parents' custody arrangement will separate you physically from one of your parents, the separation does not necessarily have to interfere with the parental influence that your parent had and will continue to have in your development. That parent might, in fact, become an even stronger influence in your life. You and your parent may learn to place an even greater value on the time you have together.

It may take added effort on the part of your absent parent and you to develop and maintain this closeness, but the effort is worth it. When this happens, you will begin to seek advice of the absent parent in positive ways. Keep in mind that some teens use the absent parent to challenge the advice or directions of the custodial parent. This is a negative way to respond to your situation and can prolong the adjustment period.

You will probably have more time alone, without either of your parents. A single parent will have a little less time, perhaps, to spread between work, home, and parental responsibilities. You will need to develop a more responsible attitude and become more independent, which are things you would probably want to be working on anyway.

New Home and Community

Your parents' divorce may mean that you have to move away from your area. This change in your life will have an impact on your friendships. When divorce necessitates a move to another town or city, it means that you will be saying good-bye to old friends. However, this does not mean that you have to say good-bye to the friendship. You will be seeing each other on your visits back home with the other parent, and you will find ways to communicate through letters or by e-mail or telephone. If your friendship is important to the two of you, you will both find a way to maintain it by keeping up with the news about what is going on in each other's worlds.

Your Parents' New Life

Adjusting to a one-parent family is a challenge in itself, but you may also be faced with an even bigger challenge, which is becoming accustomed to your parents' dating.

Dating and remarriage is probably as prevalent as divorce. Most couples do remarry after divorce. If your parents do start to see other people, or perhaps even decide to remarry, you will face many different emotional challenges. First and foremost, it may be a challenge to stay out of the middle of the developing relationship.

It is natural to look for comparisons between this new individual and your parent. On the other hand, liking this person too much might place you in that uncomfortable middle position again. One parent might question his or her child about the activities of the other parent. This places more of a burden on you as you struggle with this new life, but in time, you will learn to adjust to these new relationships.

CHAPTER 5

Lessons to Be Learned

The challenge to any relationship is how to deal with the inevitable changes that occur. Many things affect people: work, personal issues, financial issues, and family issues. Adults are constantly confronted with these challenges. Sometimes they become overwhelming and begin to cause stress in family relations.

Divorce usually begins with some kind of conflict. Regardless of how the conflict starts, some parents find it difficult to find a resolution to it. Parents may seek family or couples counseling. When they choose this route, some get the help they need either to go their separate ways or to remain in the marriage with a better understanding between them.

Important lessons can be learned from divorce. Teens can learn about conflict and how to resolve it. Teens can learn how to maintain relationships through love, caring, and support of one another. They learn about forgiveness.

Teens learn that life goes on. They learn that even if their parents are with other people, their parents' love for them will continue. Teens will find that they can adjust to the new people in their parents' lives.

Divorce can teach teens about attachments and the true meaning of family. When a family separates, it is important that the parents continue to be involved in their children's lives. If parents continue to maintain family ties, teens cannot only survive the divorce but thrive, in the process learning valuable lessons about what things are really important in life.

Resolving Conflict

Conflict is a part of life. Sometimes conflict can be resolved without much difficulty. Other times much effort will be required in order to reach a resolution. Some conflict will not be resolved. However, it is always advantageous to try to resolve conflict and almost any attempt to resolve it is beneficial. Through these attempts, individuals can learn about themselves.

Unresolved conflict between people can lead to deeper problems and greater personal dissatisfaction in the long term. Some people attempt to ease these feelings through unhealthy means such as alcohol or other substance abuse and other types of self-destructive behavior.

Conflict resolution is a skill that can be learned. Many professionals teach conflict resolution. For couples that are divorcing, these individuals are often divorce mediators. Their role is to help settle conflicts that arise from the division of property or conflicts over custody issues. Marital counselors or therapists help couples to resolve conflicts within their relationship. Any lessons you learn about resolving conflict can be applied to your future relationships.

Steps to Conflict Resolution

People find many ways to resolve conflict. There are simple steps that can be followed, however, that lend assistance to this process. The first step is laying the cards on the table.

In this stage, each party to the conflict presents his or her view of the situation. The key is that each party agrees to listen to the other's point of view about the problem without interruption. What you are trying to do is understand the other party's thinking while giving him or her the chance to understand your own. This step is preparation for reaching an agreement.

The next step is finding common ground. In this stage you are trying to find some point, no matter how small, that the two of you can agree on. The two parties have to agree to accept some degree of mutual responsibility for the conflict or problem and look for areas of compromise.

The third step is commitment. After both parties have laid their cards on the table and found some common ground, you are then ready to look for points of agreement between the two of you that will lead to commitment. Hopefully, after these steps are taken, you will be able to commit to taking actions that will resolve the disagreement or dispute and prevent future occurrences.

Relationships

Teens who have experienced the separation or divorce of their parents often show increased maturity in many ways. This maturity may stem from discovering that family security, stability, and happiness is not a guarantee and should never be taken for granted. They have also discovered that love, by itself, is not always enough to ward off disagreement and conflict.

They watched as their parents struggled with themselves and with each other in their attempts to smooth the wrinkles in their lives. As their parents formed new relationships, they had to experience adjustments that other teens did not experience. Teen children of divorced parents must adjust not only to changes in their relationships with their parents but also to the changes in their own friendships. Teens learn that you can adjust to these changes. Finally, teens learn the important lesson of forgiveness.

Through experiencing the changing nature of relationships, teens learn valuable lessons about what to expect when they are confronted with conflict or choice in their own relationships. When people are confronted with individual differences or inner conflicts, there is not always an easy answer.

Teens also learn how to adapt to the changes in their own friendships. Even though Brian stayed in his old home when his mother and siblings moved away, he was changed in some way by his circumstances. As he changed, so did his interactions with his friends. Do not be surprised if after your parents' divorce, you begin to see yourself differently. This means that you have learned something about yourself.

Spending more time with his father afforded Brian the opportunity to see his father in a different light. He came to understand the importance of cooperation. He and his father began to take the time to talk to each other about their feelings. Brian no longer felt the need to seek a family among his friends, and the nature of his friendships changed. He found himself in greater control of his actions.

Forgiveness

Another important lesson is forgiveness. Brian and Karen observed that in time their parents forgave each other. Forgiveness is important because it allows you to get rid of anger. Anger is a very destructive emotion, which causes individuals to make poor, regrettable choices. It is quite enough to witness or be involved in an environment filled with stress and conflict. Holding on to anger and resentment only prolongs these feelings and prevents the healing from taking place.

In time, Karen's mother was able to forgive her husband for the choice that he made. Though it took a long time, she was able to do it. Karen and her sister benefited by this example of forgiveness.

Karen began to see her mother differently. At first she saw her mother as weak and less capable. She was angry with her mother for being this way. Karen was also angry with her father because she felt that he took advantage of her mother. This inner turmoil caused her to sink into depression. However, when her mother began to change her own life and show her strong and capable side, Karen began to feel less angry and afraid. Her mother's strength helped them both to forgive.

Divorce does hurt. But those involved can learn many lessons from this experience. Perhaps the most

important one is that they can overcome the hurt and disappointment and they can find a new way of life.

What You Can Do

When you are in the middle of the messiness of divorce and separation, you probably will not be quite sure how to feel or what you are feeling at any particular time. But there are ways that you can gain a better understanding of these feelings. During this time, you need support.

Seeking Understanding

The first step toward healing is to seek understanding of your situation. You will need help with this; you cannot do it alone. Sometimes this help can come directly from your parents. However, in the early stages of their separation they may be too overwhelmed and unable to help you as much as you would like. This is the time to seek other resources.

Your first thought might be to talk to a relative or a friend. However, it is essential that you seek out persons who can be objective about the situation. Family members, for example, might find it hard to be objective because they are involved to some extent. There are others who will be able to listen more objectively and provide knowledgeable support.

Spending time with each parent helps to strengthen your relationships with them.

School Counselor

You might think of your school counselor only as your guide for course, college, and career planning. However, another important aspect of his or her work is personal counseling. Counselors often organize discussion or support groups for students with similar experiences and problems or can put them in touch with such groups. They have been trained in how to provide support to students who may be facing any number of problems.

The School Psychologist

The school psychologist and the school social worker are probably in your school on a periodic basis, maybe two or three times each week. However, both can be available to help you understand your feelings. They will be able to help you determine what feelings are typical in your situation, and when and whether you may need to seek other help.

The Librarian

There have been many books written on the various aspects of divorce that can help teens and younger children cope with their changing family situation. Your school librarian is a valuable resource who can help you find books on the subject. Your public library also has a wide variety of self-help titles on divorce.

These books can help you find the necessary support for understanding your circumstances.

Eventually, you will reach the point of acceptance of your parents' divorce. You will know that you and your family will survive. You will learn to trust that your parents made the best decision possible for them to make. You will learn to accept that though your life will be different, it can be shared with both your parents.

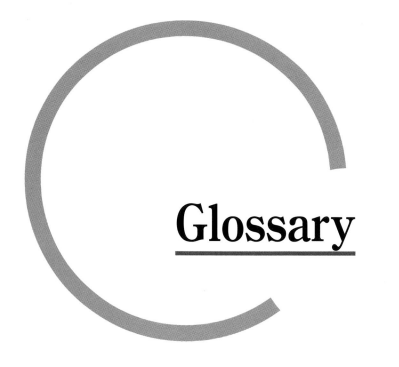

Glossary

acting out   Responding to unresolved stress or inner conflict by behaving in harmful, destructive, or uncharacteristic ways.

conflict resolution   Process of finding solutions to a dispute that minimize the destructive consequences of the disagreement and are mutually satisfactory to both parties.

custody   Literally, immediate supervision and control. In the context of divorce, custody refers to which parent is assigned the legal responsibility for raising the children of the marriage.

denial   In psychology, a defense mechanism whereby a person deals with a situation that is causing stress or conflict by denying the existence or reality of the situation.

depression   Psychological condition characterized by prolonged feelings of sadness, hopelessness, worthlessness, or despair.

divorce   The legal termination of a marriage.

grief   Long-lasting or deep distress, most often caused by a death or profound loss.

marriage   The legal and/or religious union of a man and woman as husband and wife.

physiological   Pertaining to the healthy or normal functioning of an organism.

surrogate   Substitute.

therapist   A person trained in methods of treatment and rehabilitation other than the use of drugs or surgery; especially in treatment of emotional or psychological issues.

Where to Go for Help

Children's Defense Fund
25 E Street NW
Washington, DC 20001
(202) 628-8787

Children's Rights Council
300 I Street NE
Suite 401
Washington, DC 20002
(202) 547-6227
e-mail: cdfinfo@childrensdefense.org (or go to their Web
site for regional offices:
   http://www.childrensdefense.org/contacts.html)

NEO Teenline
A confidential, judgment-free hotline where teens

can discuss their problems with caring listeners. Call (800) 272-TEEN (8336) in the United States or Canada.

Web Sites

The Kids Corner

http://eros.the-park.com/volunteer/safehaven/divorce/divorce_kids.htm
For kids whose families are going through or have been through a divorce, with links to sites specifically for teens and sites in Canada.

My Two Homes

http://www.mytwohomes.com/
A site where kids can order cool stuff to make life with two homes easier: a calendar to keep track of days with Mom and days with Dad, a handbook, a photo album, and more.

The Kids' Page at Successful Steps

http://www.positivesteps.com/Kids.htm
Lots of information and support for kids about step-families, parents, siblings, abandonment, and other subjects.

For Further Reading

American Bar Association Family Law Section. *My Parents Are Getting Divorced: A Handbook for Kids (Family Advocate)*. Chicago: American Bar Association, 1996.

Daniels Booher, Dianna. *Coping When Your Family Falls Apart*. New York: Julian Messner, 1979.

Glass, Stuart M. *A Divorce Dictionary: A Book for You and Your Children*. Boston: Little, Brown and Company, 1980.

Krementz, Jill. *How It Feels When Parents Divorce*. New York: Alfred A. Knopf, 1984.

Mayle, Peter. *Why Are We Getting a Divorce?* New York: Harmony Books, 1988.

Nightingale, Lois V. *My Parents Still Love Me Even Though They're Getting Divorced (an interactive tale for children)*. Yorba Linda, CA: Nightingale Rose Publications, 1997.

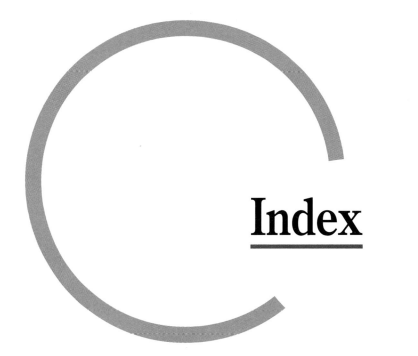

Index

About the Author

Florence Calhoun is a writer and counselor in Virginia. This is her first book for Rosen.

Photo Credits

Cover and pp. 18, 25, 27, 33, 34, 40, 42, 54, 57 by Christine Walker; p.8 by Ira Fox; p.4 by Ethan Zindler; p. 20 by Brian Silak; p. 30 © Archive Photos/ Lambert

Design and Layout

Michael J. Caroleo

Series Editor

Erica Smith